Workbook Answer Key

1 Conversation

Grammar

1

- a Eavesdropping at work can get you into big trouble! / Eavesdropping can get you into big trouble at work!
- b I had a really interesting conversation with a complete stranger recently. / I recently had a really interesting conversation with a complete stranger. / Recently I had a really interesting conversation with a complete stranger.
- c I hate people who talk endlessly about themselves all the time.
- d I overheard the most incredible conversation on the bus the other day! / I overheard the most incredible conversation the other day on the bus! / The other day I overheard the most incredible conversation on the bus!
- e I talk to my grandmother on the phone at least once a month.
- f I tried to call my boyfriend last night, but he didn't answer the phone. / Last night I tried to call my boyfriend, but he didn't answer the phone.

3

1. Earlier on in the day, I had really wanted my parents to meet my boyfriend.
2. She just didn't answer the question, frankly.
3. Later, I really regretted asking Jane to come to the party.
4. Normally, I'd just talk to him about it.
5. Jack only knew how to read Arabic.
6. Sometimes, I think she finds my obsession with neatness annoying.

4

1. b
2. b
3. b
4. b
5. b
6. a

5

1. was standing
2. was telling
3. was going
4. was always taking
5. was beginning
6. 've bought
7. 've remembered
8. 'll be getting
9. 're watching
10. had been listening
11. hadn't heard
12. were just waiting

6

- a ~~been being~~ been
- b ~~have laid~~ be lying
- c ~~might be having~~ might have had
- d ~~been understanding~~ understood
- e ~~he finally gets~~ he's finally getting / he's finally gotten

Vocabulary

1

- a animated
- b hilarious
- c frustrating
- d in-depth
- e pointless
- f lengthy
- g bizarre

2

- a get across
- b be on the same wavelength
- c flowed
- d butting in
- e drones on and on
- f hogs
- g hunt around for
- h always has something to say

3

- a skill
- b efficiently
- c competence
- d fulfill
- e satisfying
- f consideration
- g achievable

4

- a considerate
- b satisfactory
- c fulfilling
- d achievements
- e skilled
- f efficient
- g competent

Pronunciation

1

a N b A

2

- a N
- b A
- c N
- d A
- e A
- f N

Writing

1

- a The restaurant is a tapas bar that serves Spanish cuisine.
- b The atmosphere is cozy, laid-back, and friendly. It can get really busy on the weekends.
- c The restaurant is not expensive. A full meal is the same cost as an average pizza.

3

- a The review was for a movie.
- b The reader was angry as the review was very misleading. The reader expected a fun adventure movie, but the movie was sad and depressing.

4

- a 3
- b 2
- c 1

2 Taste

Grammar

1

We had a great dinner. Lucy cooked for us, and she's a fantastic cook. We started with some great little smoked salmon canapés. They were absolutely delicious! Then we had some cold cucumber soup and tiny little fingers of crisp toast. The main course was incredible; you really should have seen it. She brought out a tray of fresh lobsters and served them with a very simple green salad. I thought I couldn't possibly eat any more, but when she brought out the dessert, a home-made chocolate mousse, it was just too good to resist!

2

- a a cup of strong piping hot coffee straight from the pot
- b a mixture of tangy citrus juices with just a touch of lemon
- c a glass of ice-cold water with a couple of fresh mint leaves and a slice of lemon
- d a glass of fresh full-fat milk straight from the refrigerator
- e a steaming cup of hot chocolate with a dollop of cream on top

3

- a delicious dark chocolate
- b spicy Mexican bean
- c strong black Italian
- d exquisite hand-painted ceramic
- e large shiny red
- f tiny blue speckled
- g beautiful new china

5

- a Down came the rain and washed the dust away.
- b In the kitchen could be heard the sound of raised voices.
- c Bobbing gently on the water were half a dozen fishing boats.
- d The Western Isle was the name of the restaurant.
- e Homey, simple, and down-to-earth are the best words to describe it.
- f Long gone were the days of peace and harmony.
- g What had happened, we didn't really know.
- h When she'd be coming back, we had no idea.

Pronunciation

a cauliflower, criticism
b intricate, microwave, strawberries, vegetables
c convenience, delicious, exquisite, refreshing, selection

Vocabulary

1

a thriving
b reverie
c clientele
d GPS
e chugged
f thrust

2

a ~~informal~~ - homey
b ~~fantastic~~ - exquisite
c ~~played loudly~~ - blared out
d ~~expensive~~ - pricey
e ~~successful~~ - thriving
f ~~a mixture of flour, milk, and egg whites~~ - batter

3

a 4
b 2
c 5
d 1
e 6
f 3

4

a tasteless
b tasteful
c tasting
d tasteless

5

a bad
b acquired
c share
d accounting

6

1 That can't be right!
2 That may be, but
3 I know, it's awful, isn't it?
4 that's garbage!
5 I think you'll find that
6 Oh, I don't know,
7 I rest my case!
8 I guess you're right.

Listening

1

1 c
2 d
3 a
4 b

2

1 b
2 a, d
3 d
4 c

3

a 2
b 1
c 4
d 3

4

a on
b to
c at
d on
e on
f to
g up
h at
i up

3 City

Grammar

1

a appears; seems
b hardly any; little
c believed; recognized
d evidence; proof
e appear; seem
f proved; shown

2

a There is no doubt that smoking can lead to cancer.
b It is widely believed that climate change is the greatest challenge facing our society.
c It appears that the rate of population growth in China is beginning to decrease.
d It would seem that people believe governments are not doing enough about global warming.

3

a no
b Only
c no
d Not
e Not
f no
g Not
h Only

4

a after
b sooner
c only
d never
e after
f rarely/ seldom
g seldom/ rarely
h barely

5

a Only after I had left the city did I realize how much I loved it.
b No sooner had we moved into our new house than our troubles began.
c Not only were the local people rude to us, but they also ignored the children.
d Never had we imagined that people could be so hostile.
e Only after two months did we make our first friend.
f Rarely/Seldom did we see him, however, and life was still lonely.
g Rarely/Seldom had the children been so quiet (before).
h We decided to go back to the city. Barely had we put up a "For Sale" sign when the people began to be friendly towards us!

Pronunciation

1

a Its beauty is not as awe-inspiring as other cities.
b Everyone seems to stay out late, as though some unwritten law forbade sleeping before dawn.
c You're constantly jostled by hawkers and hordes of tourists.
d You can find pockets of another time, such as an old wooden house, a kimono shop, or a small inn.
e You might even see an old lady in a traditional dress sweeping the sidewalk outside her home with a straw broom.
f It's the city's hyperactive rush that really draws the people here.

2

~~crowded~~ dawn fog gawk
hall law ~~modern~~ ~~splendor~~
sprawl ~~world~~

Vocabulary

1

a 3
b 4
c 5
d 6
e 1
f 2

2

a magazine
b meeting
c family
d houses
e talk
f village

3

a tacky
b in-your-face
c soaring
d bustling
e haphazard
f awe-inspiring

4

a to make way for a new shopping mall
b put a finger on
c lived on top of each another
d fell prey to
e worked its magic (on me)

5

a street performers 4
b check out 5
c gorge 7
d rant 3
e gawk at 6
f handily 1
g eateries 2

6

a I really **did enjoy** the movie last night. It's one of the best movies I've ever seen.
b You're right about the new stadium. It **does look** a little bit out of place.
c Shopping malls are fine if you're looking for convenience, but I **do think** local street markets are much more interesting.
d Our neighbors are really friendly, but they **do make** a lot of noise sometimes!
e My elementary school was really small, but it **did have** an enormous sports field.
f My office is a mess. It really **does need** a good, thorough reorganization.

7

a The thing I love most about it is the dome.
b It's the way that it reflects the sunlight that I love.
c What I also like are the spectacular views from the tower.
d One thing I don't like is that you have to pay to go inside the cathedral.
e It's the square with its palm trees swaying in the wind that I love.
f What I really like is the fact that there's always a cool ocean breeze.

Writing

1

1 Furthermore,
2 For instance,
3 On the other hand,
4 However,
5 Nonetheless,

2

Suggested answers

1 ST -
2 LT +
3 ST +
4 ST +
5 LT +
6 ST +
7 ST -
8 LT +
9 ST +
10 ST +
11 ST -

4

Suggested answers

a 4
b 1
c 4
d 4
e 2
f 3
g 2
h 1

4 Story

Grammar

1

a of leaving
b to send
c to have opened
d of driving
e of signing
f to resume

2

a were going to leave way before dark
b was on the verge of giving up hope
c were hoping / had been hoping to set off by 5:30 p.m.
d wasn't going to tell him about Jack
e was originally to take / to have taken place at nightfall
f was just about to reveal everything
g (that) my parents would be a little disappointed
h was going / had been going to pay her a visit

4

a 2
b 1
c 8
d 5
e 4
f 7
g 6
h 3

5

a particularly
b Likewise
c such as; too
d To be accurate
e Strictly speaking
f or even
g that is to say; on the other hand

Vocabulary

1

a it's a long story
b tattle-tale
c cock-and-bull story
d the story of my life
e sob story
f to cut a long story short
g old wives' tale

2

a unfaithful
b astute
c gullible
d plausible
e unscrupulous
f skeptical
g fishy

3

1 f
2 c
3 g
4 e
5 d
6 b
7 a

4

a 6
b 5
c 3
d 7
e 2
f 4
g 1

5

a How awful / Oh, no. What a nightmare
b I don't blame you / I'm not surprised
c Oh, no. What a nightmare / How awful
d Lucky you / Oh, wow!
e What a relief

Pronunciation

1

a ✓
b ✗

2

a i ✗ ii ✓
b i ✗ ii ✓
c i ✓ ii ✗
d i ✓ ii ✗
e i ✗ ii ✓
f i ✓ ii ✗

Listening

1

a Della and Jim
b They are married.
c Della - her beautiful hair; Jim - his gold pocket watch
d hair combs, a gold chain for the watch

2

a 3
b 9
c 1
d 2
e 4
f 5
g 8
h 6
i 7

No, the events happened in a different order. The selling of the watch is delayed until the very end so that the reader discovers the irony of the Christmas gifts at the same time as Della.

3

a scrape together
b auburn
c flung on
d marched
e lock
f prized
g handed over
h glimpse
i trembling
j fumbled

5 Bargain

Grammar

1

Flower power
A florist in Chicago is offering bunches of dead roses wrapped in black paper for jilted lovers to send to their exes. The owner says the inspiration for the idea was her boyfriend, <u>whom she split up with last month</u>.

Security risk
A shoplifter was given a six-week jail sentence by a court in Nebraska yesterday after he removed a security tag from an item of clothing and tried to walk out of the store with it so it couldn't be used as evidence. "It's not something <u>I'm proud of</u>," Paul Gracia, 26, said as he left the court. It is the fifth shoplifting offense <u>of which Gracia has been convicted</u>.

Counting on the money
A woman from Michigan, <u>for whom Dracula and vampires have been a life-long obsession</u>, has set up a company which imports and sells coffins from Transylvania. The company sells five different products, <u>the most popular of which is painted blood red</u>.

Hitting the jackpot
A man <u>for whom the local golf club was a second home</u>, and who bought his wife a lottery ticket only to stop her complaining, has won the $500,000 jackpot. And what is the lucky Mr. Stein going to treat himself to first? "There's a new set of clubs <u>I've been saving up for</u>," he said.

2

a This is the store I got my camera from.
b Is this the hotel (which) we stayed in last year?
c Jo is someone on whom you can always rely.
d It's technically a crime, but nothing for which you'd be arrested.
e The person (who) you need to speak to is not here right now.
f Are they the people with whom Scott went on vacation?

3

a This is the store from which I got my camera. F
This is the store I got my camera from. I

b Is this the hotel in which we stayed last year? F
Is this the hotel (which) we stayed in last year? I

c Jo is someone you can always rely on. I
Jo is someone on whom you can always rely. F

d It's technically a crime, but nothing you'd be arrested for. I
It's technically a crime, but nothing for which you'd be arrested. F

e The person to whom you need to speak is not here right now. F
The person (who) you need to speak to is not here right now. I

f Are they the people Scott went on vacation with? I
Are they the people with whom Scott went on vacation? F

4

a He earns about $200 a week, most of which he spends on computer games.
b I have a few friends in California, most of whom live in Los Angeles.
c We made a lot of food for the party, most of which didn't get eaten.
d There are eight Ivy League colleges in the USA, the oldest of which is Harvard.
e We have exams all next week, the first of which is math.

5

a office; mall
b home; school
c work; school
d Tom's house; Café Coco
e café; movies
f police; government
g music of Brahms; Brahms you were playing last night
h home; school
i paella in this restaurant; paella my mother makes

6

a	the	-
b	-	a
c	-	a
d	-	the
e	the	-
f	a	-
g	the	-

Pronunciation

a /ðə/ TV remote control is on /ðə/ table.
b Is /ði/umbrella in /ðə/ hallway?
c This is /ði/ oldest building in /ðə/ city.
d Don't use /ðə/ printer. /ði/ ink's running out.
e /ði/ ice rink is next to /ðə/ park. Just before /ðə/ college building.
f /ði/ exam's on /ði/ 8th. In /ði/ afternoon.
g /ðə/ movie was great. /ðə/ scene at /ði/ end was amazing.

Vocabulary

1

a make do
b shop around
c impulse buy
d fancy meal
e down payment

3

1 get into
2 live on
3 run up
4 splashing out
5 get by
6 save up
7 cutting back
8 get around
9 came through
10 paying off

4

a the red
b cost; frills
c off; robbery

5

a broke
b discounted
c lavish
d affordable
e overpriced
f exorbitant
g frugal

Writing

• a The story is about a couple who inherited a farm and discovered a time capsule containing details about relatives that they didn't know existed.
b ii
c Jennifer's feeling about their new family 6
The business idea and how it came about 3
A brief summary of the story 1
Details of their discovery 4
The couple's plans for the future 7
Background information about Jennifer and Tyler 2
The consequences of their discovery 5

6 Mind

Grammar

1

a ~~I'm feeling~~ - I feel
b ✓
c ~~been hearing~~ - listened to / been listening to / heard
d ~~was hearing~~ - heard / could hear
e ✓
f ~~I'm smelling~~ - I (can) smell
g ✓
h ~~is tasting~~ - tastes

2

a can hear
b couldn't taste
c 'm smelling
d able to hear
e could actually see
f could smell
g can feel
h *both are possible*

3

a listening
b can hear
c can feel
d 'm feeling / feel
e could see
f smell

4

1 having spent
2 hearing
3 demanding
4 having overbooked
5 shouting and protesting
6 wanting
7 Appeased

5

a Not having understood what she'd said, he did the exercise incorrectly.
b Being American, he finds it hard to follow them when they start speaking Spanish.
c Having worked really hard at the meeting, we all went out for dinner on the company.
d Not knowing the area very well, there's a danger he'll get lost.
e Cleared / Having been cleared of theft by the court, he immediately got his old job back.

Vocabulary

1

a gaze
b examine
c recognize
d dart
e observe
f scan

2

a examined
b darting
c recognize
d observed
e scanned
f gazed

3

a ~~admit~~ - recognize
b ~~understand~~ - see
c ~~wrote~~ - observed
d ~~acknowledged~~ - recognized
e ~~remarked~~ - observed
f ~~meeting~~ - seeing
g ~~follow~~ - observe
h ~~realized~~ - recognized

4

a ramifications
b tilting
c quizzical
d barks
e sprang
f leash
g slumped

5

a up
b own
c two
d off
e out
f alike
g over
h on

6

a the last thing on my mind
b mind her own business
c of two minds
d mind over matter
e Make up your mind
f great minds think alike
g going out of my mind
h take your mind off

7

a Is it OK if I leave this until tomorrow?

- b Would you mind repeating that, please?
- c May I bring my husband with me?
- d Would you mind turning the volume down a little / turning down the volume a little?
- e Can I swap seats with you, please?

8

- a 2
- b 4
- c 5
- d 3
- e 1

Pronunciation

1

- a stimulation
- b observation
- c recognition
- d activity
- e regularity
- f creativity
- g popularity
- h perfection
- i familiarity
- j anxiety

2

- a stimulate, stimulation
- b observe, observation
- c recognize, recognition
- d active, activity
- e regular, regularity
- f creative, creativity
- g popular, popularity
- h perfect, perfection
- i familiar, familiarity
- j anxious, anxiety

Listening

1

- a Mark: work
  Kay: commuting to work
  Liza: taking care of her children
- b Mark: he finds it hard to relax after work
  Kay: she feels tired at the end of the day and often suffers from headaches
  Liza: sometimes she gets so tired she cries
- c *Any two of the following:*
  Mark: plays sports, goes running, goes to the gym, plays squash
  Kay: has a hot bath, plays some soft music, reads a book, does some cooking
  Liza: leaves the children with their grandmother, goes to a movie or art exhibition, reads the newspaper, meets a friend for lunch

2

- a Liza
- b Kay
- c Mark / Kay / Liza
- d Mark
- e Mark
- f Liza
- g Liza
- h Kay

3

- a unwind
- b fidgety
- c get away
- d pent-up
- e soul-destroying
- f drained
- g curl up
- h turning to mush

7 Digital

Grammar

1

1. light
2. business people who
3. and home
4. for a small
5. can carry
6. have to carry
7. don't want
8. Speech recognition
9. navigate your computer
10. write documents
11. you could
12. keyboard and mouse

2

Netbooks ~~are~~ inexpensive and light
~~Netbooks~~ appeal to a wide audience.
~~They appeal to~~ business people who travel frequently.
~~They appeal~~ to kids and home users.
~~They are~~ looking for a small laptop.
~~They want to be able to~~ carry ~~it~~ from room to room.
~~They also appeal~~ to students.
~~They~~ have to carry heavy books around ~~with them~~ all day.
~~They~~ don't want the extra weight of a full-size laptop.
Speech recognition has reached ~~an important~~ point ~~in its development.~~
~~With speech recognition~~ you can navigate your computer ~~without a keyboard and mouse.~~
~~You can also~~ write documents ~~without using the~~ keyboard and mouse.
~~It's much~~ faster ~~with speech recognition~~.

3

- a The perfect computer would be one that is so small and light it can fit comfortably in your pocket, but at the same time can open out to give you a full-size screen.
- b I think speech recognition could do so many good things, such as help people with physical disabilities to access all the functions on their computer quickly and easily.
- c I would love to have a car that can park itself, by lining itself up in the parking lot, and doing all that awkward maneuvering for me!

5

1. S
2. D
3. D
4. D
5. S

6

- a Sea levels are likely **to** rise by over a meter by the end of the 21st century.
- b ✓
- c ✓
- d With new advances in nanotechnology, cancer and tumors will **almost certainly** become a thing of the past.
- e ✓
- f Scientists are bound to discover~~ing~~ a cure for Alzheimer's disease by the end of the century.
- g Human beings **definitely won't** ever be able to live to more than 120.

Vocabulary

1

- a device
- b coverage
- c network
- d system
- e alert
- f voicemail
- g recognition
- h shopping
- i entertainment

2

- a wowed
- b trashed
- c went digital
- d slick
- e sold on the idea
- f hype

3

1. hype
2. wowed
3. slick
4. sold on the idea
5. go digital
6. trashed

4

- a deal
- b through
- c back
- d done; done
- e possible
- f around; around
- g sleep
- h end

Pronunciation

- a cell
- b control
- c travel
- d heating
- e touch
- f wrist

Writing

1

a, d, h

2

c

3

Paragraph *b* is the best. Paragraph *a* goes into too much detail too soon.

4

1. Not only
2. it also meant that
3. Prior to
4. But with
5. For the first time

8 The law

Grammar

1

- a In her kitchen, listening to the radio, Katie Steams heard that the radio station was giving away a free convertible.
- b What you had to do to win a convertible was answer three simple questions.

c Putting down the potato she was peeling, Katie called the radio station.
d The three questions were read (by the DJ) and Katie answered them correctly.
e What the DJ did when she went to the radio station to collect her prize was hand her a 10-centimeter model of a convertible.
f Furious, Katie decided to sue the radio station.
g Ruling in her favor, the judge ordered the radio station to pay Katie $40,000 for the real car.

2
1 would
2 must
3 should / ought to
4 would/could
5 might/could/may
6 'd/would
7 should

3
a She promised she **would** call if there were any problems.
b I'm really sorry. I **should** have been looking where I was going.
c I know I really ought **to** have called sooner, but I was really busy.
d His phone was busy. I guess he might have **been** talking to his sister.
e I thought he'd have arrived by now - he must **have** gotten stuck in the traffic.
f Why are you still working? You should **have** finished that report by now.
g You should have told me there was no food in the house - I **would** have gone to the store.
h I'm sorry, I really don't know where it is - I guess **I** might have left it at home.

4
a He's over an hour late. He must have forgotten about the appointment.
b He explained that he couldn't afford to buy a new car because it was way too expensive.
c She believes it might have been intentional.
d You should have gotten the furnace checked ...
e Cathy promised she would make sure all the doors were locked and all the lights turned off.
f They couldn't have stolen the money because they didn't have enough time.

5
a 6
b 5
c 2
d 7
e 1
f 4
g 3

Vocabulary

1
a 2
b 1
c 2
d 1
e 2
f 3

2
a sue
b arson
c The accused
d community service
e cross-examine
f return a verdict
g speeding
h libel

3
a unto
b down
c into
d above
e with
f of
g by
h against

4
a taking the law into your own hands
b in trouble with the law
c lay down the law
d above the law
e a law unto himself
f by law
g against the law
h the long arm of the law

5
a 4
b 5
c 7
d 2
e 3
f 8
g 1
h 6

6
a hear
b got
c expect
d never; thought
e tell

7
a and pigs might fly
b you can't judge a book by its cover
c still waters run deep
d wouldn't hurt a fly

8
1 c
2 d
3 b
4 a

Listening

1
a The daily allowance is less than most people earn at work.
b You can learn about how the justice system works.

2
a T
b F
c F
d F
e F
f T
g T
h F

3
a out
b off
c on
d at
e in
f off
g at
h on
i from

9 Night

Grammar

1
a however
b though
c but
d although
e even though
f though
g Despite
h yet

2
1 even though
2 though
3 despite
4 but
5 However
6 Even though
7 yet
8 Despite
9 nevertheless
10 However
11 despite
12 Try as I might
13 but
14 Saying that

4
a not having had
b had invented
c had known; would have taken
d had had; would have been
e wouldn't have lived; was going

Pronunciation

1
a *had* is pronounced as /d/
b *had* is pronounced as /d/; *would* is pronounced as /d/; *have* is pronounced as /əv/

2
a If only I**'d** gone out last night.
b I wish I**'d** had more time.
c If you**'d** been there, you**'d've** loved it.
d I**'d** like to**'ve** gone with you.
e Peter**'d've** loved it, too.

Vocabulary

1

N	D	S	U	N	S	E	T	F
M	I	D	N	I	G	H	T	S
D	B	G	K	N	R	T	J	I
A	U	Y	H	S	O	Q	L	D
W	Z	S	H	T	P	O	H	O
N	B	X	K	Q	F	M	N	A
D	A	Y	B	R	E	A	K	Y
S	U	N	R	I	S	E	L	V
T	W	I	L	I	G	H	T	L

sunset
midnight
daybreak
sunrise
twilight
dawn
noon
nightfall
dusk

2
a the middle of the night
b first thing in the morning
c last thing at night
d the crack of dawn
e mid-afternoon

3
a the middle of the night
b the crack of dawn
c mid-afternoon
d last thing at night
e first thing in the morning

4

a off
b down
c alert
d log
e light
f wink
g light
h batteries

5

1 b
2 a
3 d
4 c
5 f
6 e
7 h
8 g

6

a No, what did you have in mind?
b What are you up to this evening?
c I was wondering if you'd like to go for a drink sometime?
d That's really nice of you, but I'm going out tonight.
e No, sorry. There's something I have to do then.
f I can't make Friday, but I'm free on Saturday.

7

1 up
2 neck
3 shame
4 felt
5 up
6 time
7 mind
8 sometime
9 sounds
10 about
11 good
12 could
13 make
14 Say
15 along
16 feels
17 then
18 to

Writing

1

a yet
b Despite
c One theory
d Another theory
e However
f While

10 Footprints

Grammar

1

1 is given
2 were changed
3 is believed
4 were created
5 is known
6 are owned
7 was stolen
8 has yet to be / is yet to be
9 was sold
10 was inspired
11 was recently put / has recently been put
12 (were/are) woven
13 (were/are) set
14 had been taken / were taken
15 were placed
16 (were/are) guarded

2

a The world's most expensive shoes were made by US designer Stuart Weitzman.
b The shoes are valued at $3 million.
c The shoes are currently owned by Princess Yasmin Aga Khan, the daughter of legendary actress Rita Hayworth.
d The shoes' centerpiece is a pair of earrings once worn / that had once been worn by the actress.
e The shoes were worn by Kathleen York, a nominee, at the Oscars® in 2006.
f There is now a pair of Weitzman shoes every year at the Oscars®, and there is always great excitement about who they will be worn by.
g Several other pairs of Weitzman's shoes have been sold for over $1 million.

3

1 ever taken
2 was made
3 photographed
4 was found
5 will not be disturbed
6 is eventually eroded
7 have been made/left
8 left/made
9 having been given
10 spoken
11 is finally being discussed
12 is predicted

4

a by far
b very slightly
c just
d somewhat
e considerably
f nowhere near

Vocabulary

1

a Locally-Grown
b Renewable
c Solar-Powered
d Organic
e Energy-Efficient
f Sustainable
g Recycled

2

a 3
b 6/8
c 2
d 5
e 1
f 9
g 6/8
h 4
i 7

3

a go
b defeatist
c try
d do; good
e know; want
f twisted; arm
g happy
h point
i ventured; gained

Pronunciation

1

a Russia is <u>far</u> bigger than China.
b The book is <u>way</u> better than the movie.

2

a Computer games are <u>way</u> better than they used to be.
b The movie is nowhere <u>near</u> as good as the book.
c Canada is only <u>slightly</u> bigger than the USA.
d Soccer is <u>definitely</u> not as popular as baseball.
e The bus is only a <u>little</u> cheaper than the train.
f Computers are <u>infinitely</u> more user-friendly these days.

Listening

1

a 3
b 4
c 5
d 1
e 2

2

a 1
b 1
c 3
d 2
e 3
f helpful, relaxed, welcoming, friendly

3

Leave a minimum impact on the places you visit.

4

a hustle and bustle - lively activity
b a happening place - a place with a lot of things happening
c a well-trodden path - a route that many people take
d worth checking out - worth going to see or experience
e soak up the atmosphere - experience and enjoy the atmosphere
f watch the world go by - watch daily life happening

11 Words

Grammar

1

1 f
2 f
3 d
4 a
5 a
6 c
7 d
8 d
9 c
10 i
11 b
12 h

2

Suggested answers

A: It's Tom's 30th ~~birthday party~~ tonight. Are you going ~~to the party~~? ~~If you're going to the party~~ **If so**, I can give you a ride.

B: ~~Where is the party taking place?~~ **Where is it?**

A: ~~The party's taking place~~ At his brother's bar, I think.

B: Nobody told me anything about ~~the party~~ **it**. Maybe I haven't been invited ~~to go to the party~~. Are you going?

A: Yes. Tom invited me to the party last week when I saw ~~Tom~~ **him** at the golf club. We were ~~both at the golf club~~ **there** with our bosses. ~~Our bosses~~ **They** play golf together every Thursday.

B: I didn't know ~~your boss played with Tom's boss~~ **that**. How long have they been ~~playing golf together every week~~ **doing that**?

A: ~~They've been playing together~~ For as long as I can remember. Anyway, ~~going~~ back to Tom's party, you should definitely come. I'm sure Tom will be disappointed if you don't ~~come to his party~~. I'll see you ~~at Tom's party~~ **there**.

Pronunciation

A: ~~Are you~~ ready to go out?
B: No, not yet, ~~I'm~~ just finishing this piece of work.
A: OK, ~~we'll~~ meet you there, then.
B: Yeah, ~~I'll~~ be there in about half an hour.
A: OK. ~~We'll~~ catch you later!

A: ~~Did~~ you see John last night?
B: No, was he supposed to be there?
A: ~~As~~ far as I know, yes.
B: Hmm. ~~He~~ must have gotten caught up at work or something.
A: ~~I~~ guess so.

Vocabulary

1

a	5	d	3
b	1	e	6
c	2	f	4

2

a always connected
b lipstick effect
c credit crunch
d conspicuous consumption
e digital down time
f face time

3

a streaming
b clickbait
c catfish
d browser
e cyberbully
f selfie

4

a glean
b favor
c tangents
d rambling
e going around in circles
f got his point across
g hit the right note
h sank in

5

1 words
2 point
3 saying
4 what
5 that

Writing

1

a	✗	g	✗
b	✗	h	✓
c	✓	i	✗
d	✗	j	✗
e	✓	k	✓
f	✓	l	✓

2

a freelance translator
b He has forgotten b, c, d, e, g, i, and j

3

apply
European
trainee
went
currently
permanent
skills
from
experience
interview

4

a I'm writing to ...
b I am currently looking for ...
c I think your company will benefit from ...
d I am available for an interview ...

12 Conscience

Grammar

1

a	4	e	1
b	3	f	2
c	7	g	6
d	5		

2

a ~~join~~ - joined
b ~~spent~~ - spend
c ~~don't~~ - didn't
d ~~wouldn't be~~ - weren't/wasn't
e ~~can~~ - could
f ~~not do~~ - didn't do
g ~~would do~~ - did
h ~~might give~~ - gave

3

a It's time the town did something about the traffic.
b I'd rather you didn't speak so loud in my car.
c It's high time someone taught him a few manners. He's very rude.
d It's about time he stopped wasting time and got a job.
e I'd rather you stayed at home and took care of the children so that I can/could go shopping.

Pronunciation

1

a bungee
b sister
c fun
d thinking

The stress falls on these words because the responses are correcting a misunderstanding in the first sentence.

2

a	Relief	d	school
b	clothes		
c	brother		

Vocabulary

1

a wino - 2
b beggar - 3
c street person - 1

2

a reunited
b secure
c addressing
d pursue
e represent
f boost

3

a a clear
b on her
c In good
d ease my
e a guilty

4

a I'm really sorry. It won't happen again.
b I think I owe you an apology.
c Sorry, I had no idea this was your seat.
d I'm sorry, it totally slipped my mind.
e I really am sorry. I had no idea.
f We regret to inform you that all trains have been canceled due to bad weather.

5

a	2	d	6
b	4	e	5
c	3	f	1

Listening

1

a 1985
b to raise funds for victims of a famine in Sudan and Ethiopia
c it was first set up by comedians (and it uses comedy and laughter to get its message across)
d Red Nose Day
e fun runs, sponsored silliness, red-themed parties, role-reversal events

2

b, d, and f

3

a devastating
b refugee
c good
d catchy
e role
f organized
g silly

ISBN 9786685732245